Dumont d'Urville airstrip, Antarctica, 1989.
Steve Morgan.

GREENPEACE

WITNESS

TWENTY-FIVE YEARS ON THE ENVIRONMENTAL FRONT LINE

INTRODUCTION BY THE DALAI LAMA

WITHDRAWN

André Deutsch

State Capital Building, Lansing, Michigan, USA, 1988.
Joseph Arcure.

First published in Great Britain in 1996 by

André Deutsch Limited

106 Great Russell Street

London WC1B 3LJ

Compiled by Mark Warford

ISBN 0 233 99024 0

Cataloguing-in-Publication data

for this title available from the British Library

Book and jacket design by Senate

Printed and bound in Great Britain

by BPC Hazell Books Ltd

A member of The British Printing Company Ltd

FERNANDO PEREIRA,
Greenpeace photographer killed during the bombing
of the *Rainbow Warrior*, 10 July 1985.

This collection of images is dedicated to
Greenpeace activists and campaigners
around the world, on land and sea,
without whom this book could not exist.
Your tireless dedication to preserving
this planet is an inspiration
to us all.

Mark Warford would like to thank the following:

Daryl Upsall for his faith in the project.

Blair Palese and Cindy Baxter for a careful read.

Jay Townsend for the objective view.

Aled Davies for the signature.

Paul Whitington for his creativity.

Chloe Fletcher and Liz Somerville from the Greenpeace Communications Library.

John Novis and Erini Rodis from the Greenpeace Communications Photo Technical Department.

Steve Morgan for being there no matter what the weather.

Tom Rosenthal and all at André Deutsch for their involvement and support.

Stephanie Goodwin for her patience and for taking the call.

Stuart Brill at Senate for letting the pictures breathe.

And finally, all the photographers around the world that have endured
the best and the worst and still managed to get the picture.

INTRODUCTION

I chose to write this introduction for my friends at Greenpeace to demonstrate how important I consider the environmental issue to be. At one time, I was completely ignorant about the threat to our environment, but my eyes were eventually opened through greater awareness and my meetings with specialists in this field. The dangers facing us with regard to the environment are many and varied but most notable in my eyes are the population explosion and the advance of technology, which has now reached such a level that it is greatly disturbing nature's delicate balance.

Unless we begin to take serious notice and care of the environment today, future generations will inevitably suffer. Even now, around the world, people's lives are being affected by pollution. The problem confronting groups such as Greenpeace is that damage to the environment takes a long time to become evident. When a war breaks out, for example, the bloodshed and destruction it causes are immediately apparent. Environmental damage, however, is less visible, and great destruction can gradually occur before our very eyes without our noticing it at all. By the time we eventually realise what's happening, it will be far too late. So it is vital that we act now and develop a more caring, custodial attitude to our environment and make that attitude a central part of our lives through education and awareness.

I believe that it is essential to inform the people of the world, to impress upon them the importance of this issue and how serious the consequences of inaction could be in the future. In this regard, environmental movements like Greenpeace are invaluable, though I also feel that every single individual has a responsibility to look after our planet – it is, after all, our home. As in every human endeavour, the impetus for change must come from individuals, but individuals have to work together to make a movement effective.

Pressure groups like Greenpeace are performing an inestimable function in that they have taken upon themselves a special responsibility for our precious ecology and environment. I certainly very much appreciate their commitment and their spirit.

In 1992, I attended the Rio Earth Summit and, as I said at the time, I feel it was a very positive and important event. However, it would have been wrong to expect great changes to come in its wake, and that has evidently not happened. The summit did manage to raise awareness of the environment around the world, but unfortunately many of the participants were motivated solely by national interests and not by the interests of the group as a whole. This may be understandable, but must now be made an outdated principle. The world has become a much smaller place, and the time for thinking only of one's own little country, or even continent, has long gone. Environmental problems around the world are everyone's problem now, from which every nation can expect to suffer. However, increasing awareness with a global environment summit is at least a good beginning.

While I was at the summit, I managed to visit the *Rainbow Warrior*. It's a small boat, a little untidy. But it's a very powerful symbol, and the spirit on board is impressive. I was very inspired by that feeling, and it made my spirit stronger too.

The Dalai Lama, July 1996

It began in an unlikely place, created by three men who wanted nothing more than to do something, to somehow make a difference. Employing the Quaker tradition of bearing witness, they and others attempted to take a boat to a nuclear test site and so started what was to become the largest environmental movement in the world.

The focus of their attention was Amchitka. Situated near the western end of the Aleutian Island chain, which arcs away from the coast of Alaska and into the icy waters of the Arctic, Amchitka seems isolated from the cares of the world. But Amchitka is in the middle of one of the most earthquake-prone regions in the world, and that region had recently received a devastating reminder of the power that a severe earthquake can unleash. In 1964 a massive quake, registering between 8.3 and 8.6 on the Richter scale, had rocked the area, ripping a path of destruction across Alaska, killing 115 people, making thousands homeless and destroying 75 per cent of the state's commerce and industry. Tsunamis crashed into the shores of Oregon, California, Hawaii and Japan. Ten thousand after-shocks battered the region for the next eighteen months.

A few years later, the US government decided that its remoteness made Amchitka the perfect site for testing nuclear weapons. The decision was not popular. On the day of the first scheduled test – a one-megaton explosion, scheduled for detonation on 2 October 1969 – over 10,000 protesters blocked the major border crossings between the United States and Canada to register their concern. 'Don't Make a Wave', read their placards, 'It's Your Fault If Our Fault Goes.'

In the event, there was no earthquake. There were no tremors, no tidal waves crashing on the shore. But in a sense that didn't matter. There was a broader principle involved. The Vietnam War was reaching its climax, and anti-war sentiment was building. There was a growing sense of irritation at the arrogance of the military, at its seeming indifference to the lives and feelings of ordinary citizens. Already it was sending thousands of young men to die in the jungles of South-east Asia; now it was commandeering an island in the middle of an earthquake zone to blow up nuclear weapons. By the time the US announced plans for another blast two years later, momentum had built for a new series of protests. Jim Bohlen and Irving Stowe were Americans who had both left their homeland, depressed and disillusioned about the war in Vietnam and the nuclear policies of the US government, and had settled in Vancouver, British Columbia. Opposed to the tests at Amchitka, but frustrated by the lack of protest from established environmental organisations, Stowe and Bohlen looked for an alternative outlet for their energies. Stowe had introduced Bohlen to the Quakers, who believe in a form of protest known as bearing witness: expressing opposition simply by turning up and being seen at the site of the activity to which they object.

Recalling a Quaker ship which, in 1958, had generated publicity by sailing to Bikini atoll to try to stop a nuclear test there, Bohlen, Stowe and Paul Cote formed the Don't Make a Wave Committee, with the sole purpose of bearing witness to the Amchitka blast and bringing it to a halt. The exact circumstances surrounding the movement's change of name are uncertain, but it soon became clear that the words Don't Make a Wave Committee did not generate enough interest. What was needed was a short, catchy name which encapsulated the group's twin concerns of pacifism and environmentalism. According to one account, someone signed off one of the group's planning meetings by saying 'Peace'. Bill Darnell, a Canadian social worker, offered that it should be a green peace. Greenpeace was born.

Greenpeace chartered a 24-metre halibut seiner, the *Phyllis Cormack*, to travel to Amchitka. On 15 September 1971, the boat headed for the test site. To ensure that the voyage would generate media attention, the first Greenpeace expedition carried several journalists, including Robert Hunter of the *Vancouver Sun*, Ben Metcalfe of the Canadian Broadcasting Corporation and Bob Cummings, a reporter for the *Georgia Strait*, as well as its own photographer. On their second day, they went ashore at a Kwakiutl village, where they were given a special blessing and invited to return on their voyage home, when their names would be carved on the tribe's totem pole. Robert Hunter had taken on board a small book of Indian myths and legends. It contained one striking passage. There would come a time, predicted an old Cree woman named Eyes of Fire, when the earth would be ravaged of its resources, the streams poisoned, the deer drop dead in their tracks. Just before it was too late, the Indian would regain his spirit and teach the white man reverence for the earth, and together they would become the Warriors of the Rainbow.

Crew of *Phyllis Cormack*, Vancouver, Canada, 1971. Robert Keziere.

On 30 September, as the crew neared Amchitka, the *Phyllis Cormack* was arrested by the US Coastguard cutter *USS Confidence* for failing to clear customs during an unscheduled stop in the waters of a nearby island. The Coastguard ship escorted the Greenpeace crew away from Amchitka to clear customs elsewhere. The US government had meanwhile announced that the test would be delayed, possibly by over a month. By that time the seas around Amchitka would be rough and dangerous, and there were concerns that tensions among the Greenpeace crew would reach boiling point after so long at sea. The *Phyllis Cormack* reluctantly headed back to port. The bomb was eventually detonated on 6 November. Greenpeace had not stopped the test. But the crew had made headlines across North America, and in the process had won the battle. Amchitka was never used as a nuclear test site again.

If Greenpeace had been intended as a single-issue protest group with a limited goal, it soon began to evolve into something much larger. That one goal, after all, had been achieved; bearing witness had demonstrated its usefulness, and there were a great many other issues, beyond Amchitka, which needed to be confronted.

The US was not the only nation conducting nuclear tests, though along with Britain and the Soviet Union it had at least agreed to stop atmospheric tests and to restrict its explosions below the ground. France and China, on the other hand, had made no such commitment; in 1972, France was still exploding nuclear weapons on the Pacific atoll of Moruroa in French Polynesia. This would be the next issue for Greenpeace, and it was to launch the neophyte organisation on the international stage. Spearheading this venture was a Canadian expatriate, David McTaggart, who took up the challenge on behalf of Greenpeace.

McTaggart had a twelve-meter ketch, the *Vega*, which he sailed round the South Pacific. Outraged by the idea of the French cordoning off a portion of the ocean to explode nuclear weapons, McTaggart enthusiastically shouldered the task of taking them on.

**The *Vega*, San Francisco Bay, USA. 1990.
James Perez.**

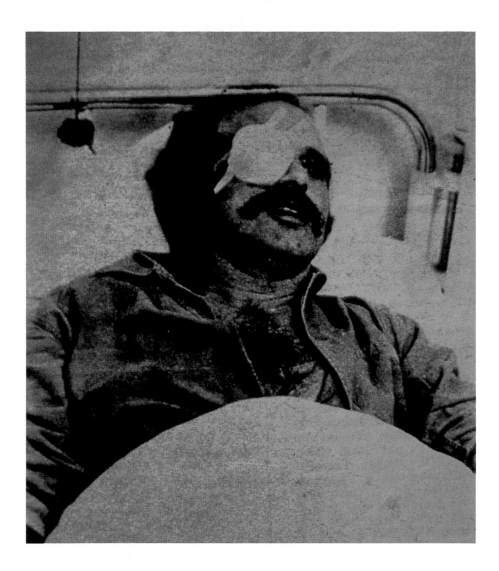

David McTaggart suffers beating by French
commandos as they board *Vega* during Moruroa
protest, Pacific Ocean, 1973. Ann-Marie Horne.

The blast was scheduled for some time in June. On 30 April, the *Vega* left port, bound for the atoll, and on 1 June, after a long and difficult journey marked by illness and crew problems, it arrived thirty-two kilometres from the test site, right in the anticipated path of the radioactive fallout from the explosion. Throughout the voyage the crew had broadcast false positions in the hope of deceiving the French, but the *Vega* had been monitored by tracking stations in Tahiti and New Caledonia. The next day, a plane flew overhead and a warship appeared nearby. For several weeks, the *Vega* held position, battling winds and waves while being constantly harassed by planes, helicopters and warships. By the middle of June, McTaggart could see, through his binoculars, a balloon hovering over the test site. The balloon was carrying the trigger device for the nuclear weapon. The test was about to take place, and the *Vega* was still directly in the path of any fallout that would occur. Undaunted, the crew elected to sail even closer to the atoll.

The following day, another French warship appeared following the *Vega*, three days later it was joined by a third, then a fourth. For eight days the three ships bore down on the *Vega*, cut across its bows and squeezed the tiny yacht between them. Finally, when the crew attempted to sail yet closer to the atoll, one of the French ships rammed the ketch. The *Vega* was crippled, and McTaggart had no option but to allow it to be towed into Moruroa for repair. There, the French military made a show of treating the *Vega*'s crew to a banquet dinner, while a photographer surreptitiously recorded the event. Although delayed by McTaggart's actions, the test was conducted as planned, and photographs of the dinner, released by the French, gave the impression that the authorities and the crew of the *Vega* were on the best of terms. Those photographs effectively negated the favourable publicity McTaggart's actions had received worldwide, and were a salutary reminder to the young organisation of the power of pictures in spreading a story in the media.

Determined to make amends, McTaggart returned to Moruroa in 1973. This time, the French wasted little time in dealing with him, boarding the *Vega* and beating him so severely that he was partially blinded in one eye. Unknown to them, however, one of the *Vega*'s crew had photographed the beating and was able to smuggle the film ashore. News of the protest and of the beating was reported around the world.

James Bay and *Phyllis Cormack*, Sidney,
British Colombia, Canada, 1976.
Rex Weyler.

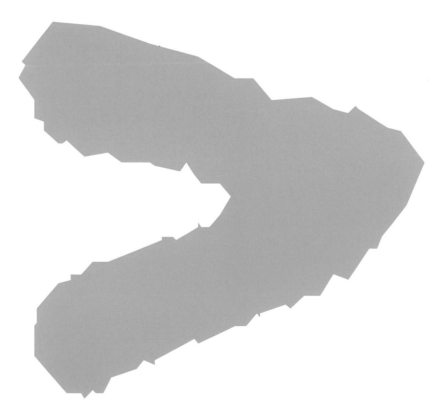

In 1974, France announced an end to atmospheric nuclear tests. But underground tests on the atoll were to continue; for over a decade, confrontation over the issue between France and Greenpeace rumbled in the background, the *Vega* returning year after year to take on the French navy until eventually it exploded to the surface, taking a life and creating a scandal that nearly brought down a government.

It was in 1975 that Greenpeace launched the campaign that was to win worldwide attention. Ironically the tactics used, which provided some of the most enduring images of the environmental movement, were inspired by those employed by the French to harass the *Vega*. For years, there had been widespread concern about the unchecked commercial hunting of whales. Population after population had crashed to near-extinction as a result of centuries of rampant over-hunting. The International Whaling Commission (IWC), founded in 1946 to prevent further over-exploitation, had instead presided over some of the worst excesses in whaling's history. A near-unanimous call, at the 1972 United Nations Conference on the Human Environment, for a ten-year moratorium on commercial whaling had been ignored by the whaling nations. Greenpeace decided to take the fight directly to the whalers, basing their plans on film of the French buzzing the *Vega* with inflatable boats, or Zodiacs. Greenpeace would take Zodiacs and place themselves directly between the whales and the harpoons. The first target was a Soviet fleet hunting sperm whales in the North Pacific. In April 1975, flying the flag of the United Nations, the *Phyllis Cormack* and the *Vega* set sail from Vancouver, cheered on by an estimated 23,000 people who had gathered at an abandoned airbase near the heart of the city.

John Sprange and Gerd Leipold at press conference following balloon flight across the Berlin Wall to protest continued nuclear testing, Berlin, Germany, 1983. Paczensky.

Finding the whalers proved more difficult than anticipated and, after several weeks without success, the ships were in need of some help. It came from Paul Spong, a New Zealand-born whale researcher who had been the motivating presence behind the whale campaign. Spong, his wife and young daughter travelled to Norway to visit the International Bureau of Whaling Statistics. Posing as a scientist interested in conducting sperm whale research in the Pacific, Spong was granted access to maps of the whaling grounds. The Greenpeace vessels had been searching too far north; Spong relayed the information back to Canada, and at the end of June 1975 the *Phyllis Cormack* found the Soviet fleet about eighty kilometres west of Eureka, California. The Greenpeace ship set off in pursuit of a whale catcher which was chasing three whales. Zodiacs were deployed to place themselves between the whales and the harpoons. As one of the Zodiacs pounded through the waves ahead of the catcher, there was a loud crack and a harpoon flew over their heads. The harpoon cable lashed a few feet away from the activists and the harpoon itself plunged into the back of a nearby whale. Greenpeace had been unable to save that whale, but the footage of the harpoon being fired so close to them became the defining image of the campaign. The *Phyllis Cormack* returned to California to a hero's welcome, and Greenpeace had found the campaign that would bring it its strongest and most widespread support, the campaign that in many people's eyes would define it more than any other.

A pattern had been established. On none of the Greenpeace voyages had the vessels or crew succeeded in their immediate aim of stopping nuclear tests or saving whales. But by being on the front line, by putting themselves in danger and, most importantly, by bearing witness to the activities of those they were protesting against, they were able to capture the imagination of people around the world. For the first time, a global public was not only becoming aware of ecological problems, it was seeing a group of dedicated, idealistic individuals who were prepared to act irrationally, some might say irresponsibly, to drive home the message about those problems, and to try to do something about them.

As Greenpeace attracted attention, volunteers and members, its ambitions grew. Under the aegis of David McTaggart, the various semi-autonomous Greenpeace groups in Europe and North America were knitted together in a formalised structure within Greenpeace International, complete with a five-member Board and national office directors. In 1976, protesters took on the Canadian harp seal hunt, inviting arrest by using their bodies as shields to protect the white-coated pups from the clubs of the fur hunters. In 1980, activists Dexter Cate and Patrick Wall were jailed for freeing hundreds of dolphins scheduled for slaughter in Japan. Other Greenpeace campaigners targeted toxic pollution and radioactive waste dumping. In protest against nuclear testing and acid rain, activists climbed smokestacks, the Statue of Liberty in New York and Big Ben in London, deploying media-friendly banners that carried their message. They marched into the Nevada test site, flew a hot-air balloon across the Berlin Wall, and blocked toxic sludge pipes in the Mediterranean and radioactive waste pipes at Sellafield in the UK.

Behind these isolated efforts lay carefully considered campaign goals. By taking on a few representative targets and gaining international media attention, Greenpeace was able to expose the broader, underlying problems: nuclear proliferation, the over-exploitation of wildlife, toxic pollution, and more.

With most of its campaigns still conducted at sea, and with a relatively concentrated group of activists straining to extend their reach globally, Greenpeace had long stopped chartering all its vessels. In 1977, it took possession of the first ship it owned outright: the *Ohana Kai*, a fifty-metre former US Coastguard submarine chaser. First used in action against the Soviet whalers in the North Pacific, it was later deployed on a fruitless search for the American tuna fleet which was killing dolphins in alarming numbers. From there, it made its way to San Francisco, where it wound up serving as a sort of floating hotel for travelling Greenpeacers before eventually being sold for scrap.

left: *Cedarlea,* London, England.
Photographer unknown.

Bridge of Rainbow Warrior, 1978. Jean-Paul Ferrero.

Over the years, Greenpeace acquired many more ships, which generally fared better than the *Ohana Kai*: *Sirius*, *Cedarlea*, *Beluga*, *Aleyka* and *Moby Dick*; and later the *MV Greenpeace*, *Gondwana*, *Rubicon* and *Solo*. Most of them served their time on numerous Greenpeace campaigns, and some of them continue to do so. But the most famous Greenpeace ship of all, and the one which did most to spread Greenpeace campaigns far and wide, was the *Rainbow Warrior* . By 1977, Greenpeace was looking for a ship that could be used to take on whaling fleets in the Atlantic as well as the Pacific, and to lead the organisation's growing campaigns in Europe. In February 1978, with financial help from the Dutch branch of the World Wildlife Fund, the organisation completed the purchase of a 23-year-old trawler called the *Sir William Hardy* and, over a period of several months, rapidly refurbished, repainted and refitted it, giving it the new name *Rainbow Warrior* in acknowledgment of the Cree prophecy that Robert Hunter had discovered on the first voyage to Amchitka.

Rainbow Warrior, Auckland Harbour, New Zealand, 1985. Miller.

The *Rainbow Warrior* was to prove its worth on many campaigns over the years, not just in the Atlantic but around the world. Within months of being purchased, the *Warrior* was confronting Icelandic whalers in the North Atlantic. Immediately afterwards it was used to protest against the dumping of radioactive waste, before returning to the whaling campaign, this time targeting Spanish whalers, as well as the killing of grey seals in the Shetland Islands. The following year it returned to the Icelandic whaling grounds, and also campaigned against shipments of nuclear materials. In 1980, while once more protesting Spanish whaling, the *Warrior* was arrested by Spanish authorities and detained in port. For five months it remained under arrest, until a skeleton crew managed to board, start up the engine and escape with the ship to the safety of the English Channel Islands. Free once more, the *Warrior* continued to be at the forefront of Greenpeace campaigns including, in 1983 and at the height of the Cold War, its most daring action yet, steaming into the forbidden waters of Siberia to document the killing of grey whales.

In 1985, the *Warrior* set out for the Pacific atoll of Rongelap on a journey known as Operation Exodus. Between 1946 and 1958 Rongelap had been in the path of fallout from at least five US nuclear tests on the nearby atolls of Bikini and Enewetak. On 1 March 1954 a fifteen-megaton H-bomb codenamed Bravo shook Rongelap, blinding the islanders and buffeting the atoll with tornado-like winds. Shortly afterwards, the island was dusted with a radioactive snow. 'We were very curious about this ash falling from the sky,' said Mayor John Anjain. Some people put it in their mouths and tasted it. One man rubbed it in his eye to see if it would cure an old ailment. People walked in it, and children played in it. Their skin began to itch, and they began to feel sick. Some of them lost their hair. Three days later they were evacuated by the Americans, but were returned to their homes after three years. The US authorities repeatedly insisted that the island was safe, but the inhabitants knew differently. Over the years, there was an increasing number of cases of cancer and leukemia and children were frequently born with deformities or suffered from retarded growth. Eventually, after the US had refused all requests for help, Senator Jeton Anjain, the Rongelap representative to the Marshall Islands parliament, approached Greenpeace.

A little under 200 kilometres away lay Mejato, an uninhabited island which had escaped the fallout. The *Rainbow Warrior* would evacuate the entire population of Rongelap and move them to Mejato and safety. The operation took a total of four trips between Rongelap and Mejato, over a period of ten days. At the end of it, Rongelap's 300 residents, together with their furniture, belongings and about a hundred tonnes of supplies, were settled on their new island home.

From there, the *Warrior* headed for New Zealand, in preparation for a renewed campaign against French nuclear testing at Moruroa. Greenpeace had notified French President François Mitterand of the planned protest, but the government in Paris knew more about the campaign than Greenpeace realised. Already prickly about criticism of the *force de frappe*, France was especially nervous about protests at Moruroa in 1985. French Polynesia had been rocked by violent protests and calls for independence, and Paris was worried that the Moruroa voyage would become a focal point for further trouble. Greenpeace's welcome as a protector of Pacific islanders at Rongelap only exacerbated French fears.

Working quietly as a volunteer in the Auckland office, and using the name Frédérique Bonlieu, French government spy Christine Cabon had managed to infiltrate the very heart of Greenpeace's preparations for Moruroa, gathering information and sending it back to Paris, where final plans were being laid to stop the *Warrior*'s campaign in its tracks. Shortly before midnight on 10 July 1985, there was an electric blue flash in the water near the *Rainbow Warrior* and Auckland harbour was rocked by an explosion. Water gushed in to the Greenpeace ship's engine room through the gaping hole torn in the stern. Captain Peter Willcox swiftly ordered everyone to abandon ship. But photographer Fernando Pereira, worried about his cameras, called out that he was going below to get them. He was in his cabin when a second explosion went off. The *Warrior*, keeled over to starboard, lay half-submerged by the dock. Four hours later, Pereira was found dead in his cabin, the straps of his camera bag tangled around one leg.

It soon became clear that the explosions were an act of sabotage, and attention immediately focused on France. Two suspected French agents were swiftly apprehended by Auckland police, and over the following weeks evidence steadily accumulated that the decision to bomb the *Rainbow Warrior* had been made at the highest level in the French government. An official French inquiry not surprisingly exonerated the government in Paris. But two French weekly news magazines accused secret agents of the bombing, and in France and around the world the media followed up the story. Repeated denials of government involvement only increased the media determination to prove otherwise. In September a report in *Le Monde* declared that not only had the operation been conducted by French agents, but their actions had been known to Defence Minister Charles Hernu and Admiral Henri Lacoste, head of the French secret service, the DGSE. In fact, said *Le Monde*, the two men had probably ordered the bombing.

Two days later, Lacoste was fired and Hernu resigned. Rumours of involvement at the highest level proliferated. For a while, *l'affaire Greenpeace* looked like claiming President Mitterand himself. But the ticking political bomb was defused by Prime Minister Laurent Fabius. Appearing on television to admit that DGSE agents had indeed been responsible for the sabotage of the *Rainbow Warrior*, he declared that the agency had hidden the truth from the government inquiry. Fabius and Mitterand, by implication, knew nothing; Hernu, Lacoste and the DGSE were made scapegoats for the whole affair. Without enough evidence to charge the two arrested agents with arson or murder, or to show that they had been the ones who had actually planted the bombs, the New Zealand authorities were forced to strike a deal. The agents pleaded guilty to manslaughter and wilful damage and, after a trial of just thirty-four minutes, they were each given concurrent sentences of ten years on the first charge and seven on the second. Under severe political pressure from Paris, New Zealand agreed that they should serve their sentences at the French military base on Hao atoll. Two years later they were repatriated, and were later awarded medals for their service to the French republic.

The *Rainbow Warrior* was refloated, but the cost of repair would have been prohibitive. Greenpeace accepted an offer from the people of Matauri Bay, in New Zealand's Northland region, to sink the ship in their waters both as a monument and an artificial reef. On 12 December 1987, as a cluster of small boats gathered round, and Greenpeace helicopters flew overhead, the *Rainbow Warrior*'s last journey came to an end as it settled slowly in the water and then sank, bow first, beneath the waves.

With the sinking of the *Rainbow Warrior*, and the death of Fernando Pereira, everything changed. What had begun as an idealistic boatload of hippies, Quakers and peace activists had grown into a powerful political force. Far from removing Greenpeace from the scene, or even crippling its operations in any way, the bombing of the *Warrior* had invested the organisation with an identity and credibility that fourteen years of campaigns around the world were only beginning to achieve. Instead of silencing its critics, the French government actions had managed to bring Greenpeace to the attention of a wider public than ever before.

At the same time, concern over environmental issues was reaching new heights. Acid rain was destroying forests in Germany and Scandinavia. Emissions of so-called greenhouse gases such as carbon dioxide were reported to be causing a phenomenon referred to as global warming. NASA images proved to the world the existence of a hole in the ozone layer above Antarctica. The explosion of the Chernobyl nuclear reactor renewed fears about the safety of nuclear power. Seals started dying in their thousands in the North Sea, and dead and diseased dolphins washed up on the east coast of the United States. The *Exxon Valdez* spilled 11 million gallons of crude oil onto the beaches of Alaska's Prince William Sound. Dolphins, sharks, sea-birds, turtles and other wildlife were dying in their tens of thousands in huge drift nets that spread for miles across the sea. Tropical rainforests were being destroyed at the rate of thirty acres a minute. And if the end of the Cold War had reduced concern about nuclear weapons, the lifting of the Iron Curtain revealed an environment devastated by runaway pollution. In the USA, *National Geographic* magazine devoted a special issue to the fate of the global environment; and *Time* magazine forsook its annual Man of the Year award to honour the Earth as its Planet of the Year. In Britain, the Green Party won an unprecedented fifteen per cent of the vote in elections to the European Parliament.

Around the world, people flocked to give their support to the growing number of environmental organisations. The one that attracted the greatest support was Greenpeace. In the five years after the bombing of the *Rainbow Warrior*, Greenpeace's membership soared from around a million in 1985 to an all-time high of 4.8 million by 1990. It opened offices in Argentina, Italy, Ireland, Norway, Japan, Finland, the USSR, Czechoslovakia, Chile, Greece, Brazil and Tunisia. And it became the first non-governmental organisation in history to establish a permanent base on Antarctica.

Plans for a permanent presence in the Antarctic had been well under way long before the *Warrior* was sunk. For a number of years there had been growing concern over the potential threats facing what was widely regarded as the world's last true wilderness area. Barely even seen by humans before the end of the century, Antarctica remained relatively untouched. Although seven countries had lodged – sometimes conflicting – territorial claims to the continent, these had all been effectively frozen by the 1959 Antarctic Treaty. A landmark international agreement, the Treaty established that Antarctica shall be used for peaceful purposes only and promoted the continent as a site of international scientific co-operation. But beneath the layers of snow and ice lay untapped minerals, including copper, silver, gold and uranium, as well as coal and oil. With the Treaty scheduled for renegotiation in 1991, many more countries began establishing bases on the continent, in the hope of increasing their claim to the treasures that they hoped would be unlocked. In the process, they littered the fragile Antarctic environment and threatened the wildlife that eked out a tenuous existence along the coastline.

As nations began piecing together a draft minerals convention to replace the Antarctic Treaty, Greenpeace agreed to throw its weight behind existing efforts to block its adoption. The campaign soon developed from simply protesting a specific convention to promoting Antarctica as the place where the line should be drawn, the remaining area on Earth that should be beyond the reach of human exploitation. It was out of this concept of World Park Antarctica that the idea was born to establish a permanent presence on the continent.

The notion of Greenpeace having a year-round base on Antarctica was controversial within the organisation. For one thing, even though the proposed base would be extremely small compared to many of the scientific stations already in existence, it seemed to some that the whole idea ran counter to the basic thrust of the entire campaign. Even if there was an advantage to be gained from establishing a base, could Greenpeace do it? Very few private expeditions to Antarctica had ever been successful, and none had ever set up and maintained a year-round presence on the continent.

Undaunted, the organisation went ahead with the plans. In 1985, it bought a converted ocean-going tug; called it the *Gondwana* after Gondwanaland, the ancient super-continent from which Antarctica had calved; changed its mind and renamed it the *Greenpeace*; ice-strengthened the bow; and added a helicopter pad and satellite communications. Shortly after launch, the *Greenpeace* was forced to make a detour, replacing the stricken *Rainbow Warrior* at the head of the Moruroa protests, but in late 1985 the ship was ready to go and set off from New Zealand for its rendezvous with the great frozen continent. The voyage was a disaster. Sea-ice levels around Antarctica were the highest in decades; at least two ships were stuck in the ice for weeks and a third was crushed between ice floes and sunk. The *Greenpeace* avoided that fate but was unable to push through to Ross Island, the chosen site for the base, and was forced to return home.

Overwintering in Antarctica, 1990. Robin Culley.

Water sampling, Ontario, Canada, 1988. Joseph Arcure.

It seemed as if the sceptics had been right. But despite some efforts to remove the expedition and the base from the campaign, there was another attempt the following year. This time, despite some scary moments, the *Greenpeace* made it to Ross Island. Finally, in February 1987 work was complete, and Greenpeace had established World Park Base, a lurid, yellow-green hut just a few hundred yards from the base site of Scott's last expedition to the South Pole. Here, for the next five years a four-person team, changed annually, stayed year-round, making scientific observations, checking environmental conditions and keeping an eye on the nearby US and New Zealand bases in McMurdo Sound. The *MV Greenpeace* was relieved of Antarctic duty by a more sturdy ship, which was given, and this time kept, the name *Gondwana*, and the annual resupply of the base was the focal point of a series of Antarctic expeditions for Greenpeace. In 1989 the minerals convention collapsed, and in 1991 Antarctic Treaty nations adopted an Environmental Protocol which included a ban of at least fifty years on mineral exploitation in Antarctica.

With a base on Antarctica and the opening of an office in Tunisia in 1990, Greenpeace had become the first non-governmental organisation of any kind to have a permanent base or office in every continental region of the world. Its reach was now truly global; and although a combination of factors, including a worldwide recession, led to a drop in support in the first half of the 1990s, membership worldwide remained comfortably above three million.

Greenpeace's post-*Warrior* growth meant that it was now able to take on an increasing array of projects and campaigns. Building on the success of its protests against nuclear testing at Moruroa and the enormous goodwill generated by the *Warrior*'s final voyage, Greenpeace formally set up a continuing Pacific campaign to tie together the threads of nuclear, toxic and ocean ecology issues in the region. Other regional campaigns were established in the North, Baltic and Mediterranean Seas. An international waste trade project campaigned for a global ban in the trade of radioactive, chemical and biological waste products, particularly from industrialised to less developed nations. The Nuclear Free Seas campaign protested the use of the oceans by nuclear-armed navies. What had once been isolated campaigns against the killing of seals, whales, dolphins and sea turtles now evolved into a broader focus on ocean ecosystem issues, including the growing problem of global over-fishing. A new campaign was established to address growing concerns over scientific evidence that the planet's atmosphere was under siege from ozone-depleting chemicals and that human activities were even beginning to alter the climate. The organisation's interests spread inland, too, to the fate of the world's forests, and the environmental devastation in Eastern Europe and the former Soviet Union.

Greenpeace's arrival in the Soviet Union, in the waning days of the Cold War, was preceded by the release of an album, entitled 'Breakthrough'. Featuring tracks donated by such recording artists as Annie Lennox, Peter Gabriel, U2, Sting and The Grateful Dead, 'Breakthrough' was the largest pressing of Western rock music in the Soviet Union and the first charity album ever released there. Some 3 million double albums and 500,000 double cassettes were released; the first half million were sold within hours of release. The record immediately went to Number One on the official Tass news agency chart and stayed there for several months. Royalties from the album's sales were used to establish Greenpeace offices in Moscow and Kiev. Renamed 'Rainbow Warriors', the album was subsequently released in many countries.

Several years later, Greenpeace released another album, 'Alternative NRG', containing tracks recorded live on stage by various artists using a solar-powered recording studio. Greenpeace in the USA now has a Tour Project, which allows the organisation to use major rock tours as vehicles to promote its campaigns, gather signatures for petitions and distribute literature.

The post-*Warrior* era has seen the development of a greater sophistication and specialisation in Greenpeace's operations. Greenpeace Communications, the organisation's media arm, maintains contact with international media around the world, coordinates press and publicity for campaigns and actions, drafts press releases, hires photographers and cameramen to cover Greenpeace activities, and edits and distributes video and pictures for broadcast and publication on television and in magazines and newspapers. Greenpeace also had a dedicated books division (since closed) which produced publications on Antarctica, dolphins, the seas of Europe and the nuclear age, as well as two editions of an official history.

In support of its growing campaigns, Greenpeace put increasing emphasis on scientific research and analysis. Several campaigns and offices developed their own scientific expertise. Greenpeace Austria converted a bus into the most sophisticated mobile laboratory in Europe. Similarly the *Beluga*, a 24-metre former fire patrol boat bought by Greenpeace in 1984, plied the waterways of Europe monitoring pollution levels and analysing water quality. A Greenpeace Science Unit was established at Queen Mary and Westfield College, at the University of London (later moving to the Earth Resources Centre at the University of Exeter), and supporting science labs were set up in Boston and Kiev. Research generated and supported by Greenpeace is now frequently published and widely cited.

A Treaties and Conventions Project was set up to present this research to international conventions and demand action and legislation to prevent environmental degradation. This project, which later evolved into the Political Unit, deployed expert lobbyists to work with campaigners and push the Greenpeace agenda in fora as diverse as the International Whaling Commission, the London Dumping Convention, the Basel Convention (on hazardous waste trade), the International Maritime Organisation, and the Convention on International Trade in Endangered Species. Meanwhile, overseeing probably the most visible aspect of Greenpeace activities, Greenpeace Marine Services maintained the organisation's fleet of ships, interviewed and hired crew, and mapped out itineraries that took the *Greenpeace*, the *Vega*, the *Moby Dick* and the rest around the world.

As the 1980s drew to a close, Greenpeace was in a stronger position than ever before. It was now a household name. It had pioneered and perfected the technique of isolating a problem, defining a target and exposing it in the global media. In so doing, it had helped push environmental issues to the top of the political agenda in many countries, and played a significant role in fostering many changes in behaviour and attitude. The number of membership supporters and national offices around the world, as well as the growing awareness it was developing as a result of its scientific research and the success of its campaigns, gave Greenpeace an influence that its founders could only have dreamed of achieving.

But for all the success, something was missing. That missing piece was put in place on 10 July 1989, when Greenpeace's newest ship was launched in Hamburg. Sleek, 55 metres long, this converted trawler was fitted with a full rig of sails and embarked on a six-week tour of Europe before undertaking a tour of duty that would take it around the world. The ship's name reflected the important place it would have in the Greenpeace fleet: it was called *Rainbow Warrior*.

Rainbow Warrior, Tasman Sea, 1990. Roger Grace.

Korean children on *MV Greenpeace,*
Korea, 1994.
Hiroto Kiryu.

Twenty-five years after the first voyage of the *Phyllis Cormack*, Greenpeace, at least outwardly, bears absolutely no similarity to the idealistic group of pacifists and would-be whale-savers who first set to sea in the early 1970s. Administered from a central office in Amsterdam, Greenpeace has a worldwide staff of hundreds, an international board of directors and a multi-million-dollar budget. It has owned fourteen ships, two helicopters, a bus, innumerable inflatables and a hot-air balloon. Greenpeace campaigners are just as likely to be seen in suits at an international conference as in T-shirts and jeans on a ship, or climbing a smokestack. Walk the corridors of the Amsterdam headquarters (known within the organisation simply as 'international') and it is hard to imagine that you are at the centre of a cutting-edge organisation dedicated to protecting the global environment. Were it not for the photographs on the wall – scenes from various Greenpeace campaigns – it might almost be just another corporate headquarters, housed in a dramatic, stately building at the junction of two Dutch canals.

Greenpeace's diversity, despite its earlier growing pains, is now one of its greatest strengths. It gives the organisation a breadth and depth of knowledge and experience that few others can approach. With offices in over twenty countries, Greenpeace can call on a range of perspectives that enable it to articulate a genuinely global view of environmental issues. The dark-suited lobbyists who negotiate on national, regional and international agreements know that they are backed up by a front line of activists who will not hesitate to draw attention to the failings of a particular agreement; similarly, those who block pipelines, roads and rail tracks, hang banners or drive inflatables know that their actions are not taking place in a vacuum, and that there is a wealth of dedicated and experienced campaigners, media experts and lobbyists who can take the grass-roots actions and shape them as part of an organised effort to affect policies and behaviour.

That same diversity makes Greenpeace a moving target, difficult for its critics to pin down. The corporate and media attacks on Greenpeace in the early 1990s, the attempts to portray it as a nest of vipers cynically trying to coerce an innocent people out of its money, did not wash with a public that knew the organisation for its dramatic direct actions and its willingness to take risks in order to highlight environmental problems. The other angle of attack, dismissing Greenpeace as irresponsible trouble-makers looking only to foster conflict and uninterested in solutions, did not square with the fact that, at the same time as some of its members were blocking pipes or climbing smokestacks, others were acting as advisers to government delegations at international conventions, or working with industry to create environmentally safe products.

In structure and operation, Greenpeace is undoubtedly a very different organisation from the one that existed twenty-five or, for that matter, twenty or even ten years ago. Whether the changes have been for better or for worse is a largely subjective judgement, but also to some extent an irrelevant one. What is more to the point is that these changes were inevitable and essential. The world in which Greenpeace operates today is very different from the one in 1971. During those early voyages with the *Phyllis Cormack* and the *Vega*, the world at large was relatively ignorant of environmental issues. Certainly, the public had never before seen television pictures of people who cared so much about the state of the environment that they were prepared to take daring actions, apparently to the point of putting their lives at risk, to drive their message home. Those actions were enough by themselves to arouse public interest, to make people sit up, take notice and feel connected to matters ostensibly far from their immediate concerns. Twenty-five years later, that same public has grown more sophisticated and the task is more complex. Thanks in no small part

to Greenpeace and other organisations, there is a widespread understanding of environmental issues. Although the public still responds to images of Greenpeace campaigners bouncing across rough seas in inflatables, this is no longer always enough.

Accordingly, although Greenpeace agrees on its campaign priorities and policies on an international basis, the way it approaches those campaigns varies, depending on circumstances and regions. In Japan, for example, where the emphasis – officially at least – is on harmony and unity rather than the conflict and debate of the West, Greenpeace approaches issues tentatively, seeking to use discussion and persuasion rather than confrontation. In Germany, the organisation has demonstrated that environmentalism can be practical and efficient, by designing a prototype refrigerator which does not use ozone-depleting chemicals and which is now being taken up by all large manufacturers. In the United States, where the potential for compassion fatigue looms largest and the list of social ills is longer than in many other countries, Greenpeace emphasises environmental justice, underlining the links between environmentalism and human equality and demonstrating, for example, the prevalence of dirty industries in poor, urban neighbourhoods. The effectiveness of Greenpeace's multi-pronged approach is easily demonstrated by a sample list of the successes that the organisation has managed to achieve in this decade alone: the adoption by the Lome IV Convention of a ban on the import of radioactive waste by contracting parties in Africa, the Caribbean and the Pacific; the World Bank's adoption of a forest policy prohibiting Bank financing of logging in primary tropical forests; the agreements by German industrial giant Hoechst, the world's largest producer of ozone-depleting substances, to stop producing CFCs sooner than any other company in the world and, later, to end production of chlorinated paraffins; the decision by furniture maker IKEA to stop using PVC in its furniture; a worldwide ban on large-scale drift net fishing; the announcement by Russian President Boris Yeltsin of a Commission on Inquiry to investigate Russian radioactive waste dumping, after years of repeated Soviet and Russian denials that such dumping took place; the agreement by parties to the Barcelona Convention to phase out discharges of all toxic, persistent and bio-accumulative substances into the Mediterranean by 2005; the adoption by the International Whaling Commission of a Southern Ocean Whale Sanctuary; the decision by the French government to scrap plans to build a hard-rock airstrip on Antarctica; the adoption by governments of the Washington Declaration, calling for a global treaty to restrict persistent organic pollutants; and the agreement by parties to the Basel Convention to ban the trade of hazardous waste from developing countries to less developing countries.

These are just a few of the more notable successes for which Greenpeace can claim at least partial credit in recent years. By their nature, because such victories are more tangible, they primarily reflect Greenpeace's work at international conventions. Less easy to document, but far more common and in their way even more effective in the long term, are the innumerable smaller successes in raising awareness and gaining converts that Greenpeace achieves around the world every day: the campaigner who talks to a group of schoolchildren, possibly inspiring some of them to take an active role in protecting his or her local environment; the door-to-door fundraiser who convinces the sceptical home-owner; the family watching a Greenpeace spokesperson making his or her point on national television. Measuring those achievements is no easy task, but they are every bit as valuable as the passage of resolutions or the adoption of legislation, in that, bit by bit, piece by piece, they help inform, educate and shape people's attitudes to the world we live in.

Greenpeace today is often at its most effective when it is able to combine its various elements – public awareness, media expertise, direct action and political lobbying – into one package in such a way that the whole far exceeds the sum of the parts. There are many examples available. Just one is Greenpeace's campaign in support of a 1992 French proposal that the International Whaling Commission (IWC) should declare the waters around Antarctica as a sanctuary for whales. It was an important step, both as a safeguard against the possibility of resumed commercial whaling (an IWC-mandated global moratorium had been in effect, although much violated, since 1985) and as a symbolic gesture. In the same way that World Park Antarctica had succeeded because people had responded to the idea that the Antarctic should be off limits, so it seemed certain that there would be a positive reaction to the argument that, after all the exploitation endured by the great whales of the Southern Ocean, it was time we preserved their most important habitat. Just because we could exploit them, it didn't mean that we should.

Not everyone agreed. Most governments were reluctant to take that step and even many environmentalists were at first dubious about the plan, thinking it unnecessary with a moratorium already in place. But even in the face of intense lobbying against the proposal by Japan and other pro-whaling governments, Greenpeace was able to deploy a varied arsenal in support of its case. Its direct actions and expeditions to Antarctica had produced footage which was used to show the natural beauty of Antarctica, and contrasted with scenes of whales being killed there. Its scientific experts and advisers helped provide evidence to demonstrate the need to protect the remaining whale stocks. Campaigners around the world worked tirelessly to drive the message home and gather popular support. The effort was spearheaded by Greenpeace's political team, lobbying governments and IWC representatives whenever and wherever possible. The combined offensive proved instrumental in turning opinion in support of the proposal. At its annual meeting in 1994, the IWC voted overwhelmingly to adopt the Southern Ocean Sanctuary.

Minke whale and Japanese catcher ship, Southern Ocean, 1992. Robin Culley.

Brent Spar, North Sea, 1995. Harald Zindler.

Later that year, when the Japanese fleet set sail for the Antarctic anyway, Greenpeace gave chase. Early in 1995, the *MV Greenpeace* caught the whalers in the act four times; the media and public responded with outrage to the fact that the fleet were not only killing whales but were doing so in the new Southern Ocean Sanctuary. Five countries lodged formal objections with Japan. It was a classic example of how Greenpeace's lobbying, media and direct action campaigns worked together to maximum possible effect.

That same year, Greenpeace dominated the headlines in ways that it had not done for some time. In the North Sea, bearing witness bore fruit dramatically as Greenpeace protested the proposed dumping at sea of the disused Shell oil platform, Brent Spar. For weeks, Greenpeace activists boarded and occupied the platform as it was being towed to its proposed burial site; as the action built up, so did a public campaign of support in Britain, Germany and elsewhere until eventually Shell conceded and agreed to find alternative means of disposal. Arguments from opponents that the environmental risks posed by dumping that one rig were minimal, or disagreements about the amount of oil still on board, missed the point. Greenpeace's campaign gained such public momentum because, in its strongest tradition, it had taken a specific case and used it to highlight a broader issue: that governments and industries were behaving in too cavalier and irresponsible a fashion towards the global commons, using international waters as the dumping ground for their wastes. On an intuitive level, the European public knew that that was wrong, and reacted to the Brent Spar campaign accordingly.

Even as the organisation was still buzzing from the Brent Spar success, it was gearing up to fight the decisive battle over its longest-running issue. After a decades-long arms race, worldwide political pressure was building for a permanent ban on the testing of nuclear weapons. Unfortunately, newly elected French President Jacques Chirac chose to announce his arrival in office with a new series of tests at Moruroa. The *MV Greenpeace* and the *Rainbow Warrior* headed a flotilla of ships and boats to the test site, once more using the organisation's resources to bring attention to what was happening in a remote part of the world. French commandos boarded and seized the Greenpeace ships, but by then the damage had been done, and the criticism could not be silenced. In Tahiti, news of the tests provoked riots; in France, Chirac's popularity plunged. Eventually, the French President brought the tests to a premature halt and announced his government's support for a Permanent Test Ban Treaty. After several difficult years Greenpeace was back to its best, still a force to be reckoned with.

Nuclear testing demo, Tahiti, 1995. Steve Morgan.

Working for Greenpeace carries its risks and frustrations. Greenpeace ships have faced all manner of attack, their crews have been shot at and arrested. Campaigners are regularly vilified in the media and subjected to personal abuse. Canvassers spend long evenings trudging from door to door, trying to convince people to support the cause. There are many times when you feel like a cog in a giant wheel, when you wonder if you are really making any difference. It seems to take an age to lobby for a particular piece of legislation, to write a report, to pull together a direct action. Then the legislation is passed, the report is published, the action is over, and you wonder: have I really made any difference? There are many times, after long days of writing, telephoning, meeting and perhaps receiving the occasional abusive phone call, or putting out the brush fire of an inaccurate media report, when you wonder if it is all worth it. Whales are still being killed, oceans are still being polluted and over-fished, there are still enough nuclear weapons to annihilate humanity several times over. But then you remember the positive aspects: letters and drawings from schoolchildren; people shaking your hand when you tell them you work for Greenpeace; the occasional recognition that the issue on which you have worked so long has seeped into the public consciousness.

Bearing witness works because it pulls people in to an issue; makes them feel that they could be there even when they're not; helps them feel empowered, a part of something; and reassures them that, even if they can't block pipelines, occupy an oil rig or drive in front of whaling ships, they are giving their support to those who can do these things on their behalf. It enables us all to share in the effort to keep the world that little bit greener, safer and more peaceful.

Greenpeace was not the first organisation to draw attention to environmental problems, nor will it be the last. But it has highlighted those issues and mobilised public response around the world in a way no other organisation has achieved before. Ultimately, the answer to the question posed by those of us who have doubted our efforts, wondered if it was all worth it, is a resounding Yes. Not because of the whales we did or did not save, the nuclear tests we did or did not prevent, or the toxic waste shipments we did or did not stop, but because all those things – successes and failures alike – have helped build an ever-growing sense of awareness of the many complex environmental issues we face.

In the process, Greenpeace has helped create something that is far bigger than all the individuals involved, that will outlive them all and even Greenpeace itself: a growing global community, environmentally aware and willing to make a stand and be heard, in its quest for a green and peaceful planet.

Kieran Mulvaney

Ocean dumping, North Sea, 1982. Pierre Gleizes.

"It's not intended to be a suicide operation!

Accidents like this are the last thing we want. We had practised with two or three people in the boat – even then it was very, very dangerous – but once I had volunteered to do it I knew I would be completely alone.

When I came alongside the ship I was trying to watch the guy who was pulling the rope which basically released the hook – one second not looking and that's it!

The barrels landed in the front of the boat and I fell out of the back. I banged my head on the engine on the way but luckily somebody pulled me out of the water within twenty seconds. I was just freaked out! When I returned to the ship I was shaking and crying; all kinds of emotions were surfacing, and my overall feeling was that somehow I had made a mistake or jeopardised the organisation."

Gijs Thieme

"The situation in the Mediterranean Sea at that point was quite volatile.

The American Sixth Fleet was present and a number of Russian nuclear submarines and ships were also in the area; we were very concerned. It was suggested that someone should climb the anchor chain and I was asked if I would do it. My initial anxiety was with fixing myself to the chain because, if they let go of it, it would travel to the sea bed very quickly and I would have no time to get off... But we were exploring the possibilities.

I saw that the best way for me to climb was with bare feet because then I would actually be able to feel the links and use them to step up the chain.

I was ferried over in the inflatable and the two people with me tied their boat to the chain as I got down to business, scrambling up as quickly as I could. It was all very hectic! The captain was in constant contact with the ship, informing them of the non-violent nature of our actions, but we can never predict their reaction. In fact the fire hoses were turned on me straight away, but I was very focused. I'm totally opposed to nuclear development, so I knew exactly why I was there.

Sure enough, they started to lower the chain, which was very frightening. I realised that I would have to get off very quickly because the boat that was tied to it was getting dragged under the water, as you can see in the picture. For safety reasons I had no option other than to jump off. But we had delivered our message!

Grace O'Sullivan

Campaign for nuclear-free seas, Mediterranean Sea, 1989.
Mike Midgley.

MV Greenpeace, Southern Ocean, 1993.
Marty Lueders.

Toxic sludge dumping, Mediterranean Sea, 1995.
Steve Morgan.

The Rongelap evacuation was certainly the most impressive thing I did in my 11 years with Greenpeace.

It wasn't a direct action; it wasn't a matter of tying up banners. When we got to that village and saw churches and buildings we realised that people had been living there for generations and were about to give it all up, and it became much more serious than anything we'd done before.

The islanders didn't feel safe bringing up their children in that environment. For the thirty years after the US nuclear testing had been carried out they had been living on Rongelap and seeing personal health deteriorate; women had multiple miscarriages, children were deformed at birth or mentally retarded and, when we were there, well over 95% of the people present at the time of the explosion had thyroid cancer. The US and Marshall Islands government had turned down flat their appeal to be moved.

Having to relocate 350 people across 120 miles of sea was a huge undertaking as we were on a tight schedule to get to New Zealand and then back out to Moruroa. Looking back on it, if we had taken another week or two we could have done more for them... But there was a good feeling and they were very grateful."

Pete Willcox
Captain, *Rainbow Warrior*

Rainbow Warrior, 1980.
Pierre Gleizes.

*Rongelap evacuation,
South Pacific*, 1985.
Fernando Pereira.

Ocean incineration campaign, North Sea, 1987.
Lorette Dorreboom.

Protest against
ICI, London,
England, 1992.
Jim Hodson.

Petition delivery
against French
nuclear testing,
Paris, France,
1995.
Pierre Gleizes.

Whaling campaign,
North Pacific, 1978.
William Mosgrove.

Campaign against
Russian whaling, 1975.
Rex Weyler.

Campaign against Russian whaling, 1975.
Rex Weyler.

Removal of World Park Base, Ross Island, Antarctica, 1992.
Tim Baker.

Palmer's Island, Antarctica, 1988.
Steve Morgan.

Campaign against
Russian whaling,
1975. Rex Weyler.

Outflow sampling, Whitehaven, England, 1990.
Alan Grieg.

Spain, 1978.
Peter Lagendyk.

Campaign against Russian whaling,
1975.
Rex Weyler.

Dolphin slaughter, Iki Island,
Japan, 1980.
Susie Cate.

John Johnson.

Activists during chlorine blockade,
Vancouver, Canada, 1990.

Roger Grace.

Launching Greenpeace balloon,
USA, 1987.
James Perez.

USS Kittiwake rams MV *Greenpeace*, Florida, USA, 1989. Jay Townsend.

Damage to *MV Greenpeace* following ramming by *USS Kittiwake*,
Florida, USA, 1989. Robert Visser.

overleaf:
French Commandos storm *Rainbow Warrior*,
Moruroa, South Pacific, 1995.
Steve Morgan.

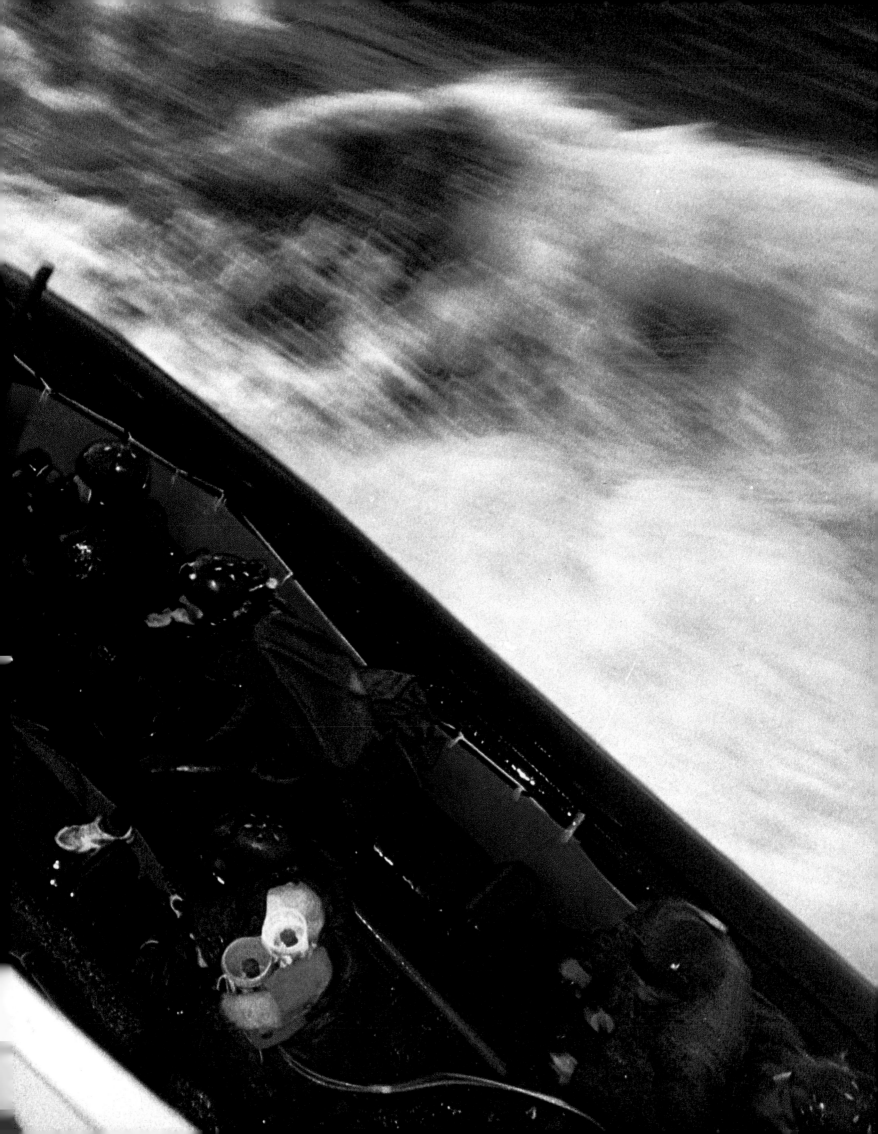

Ted Hood, Southern Ocean, 1992.
Marty Lueders.

Pipe block, Cumbria, NW England, 1991.
Richard Smith.

HMS Ark Royal,
Hamburg, Germany, 1989.
Dieter Vennemann.

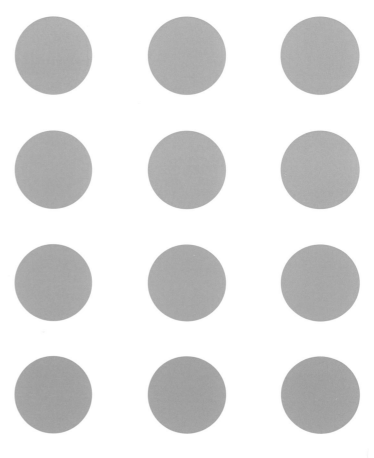

Beluga tour, USA, 1988.
Sam Kittner.

Dolphin in drift net,
Azores, Atlantic, 1991.
Peter Rowlands.

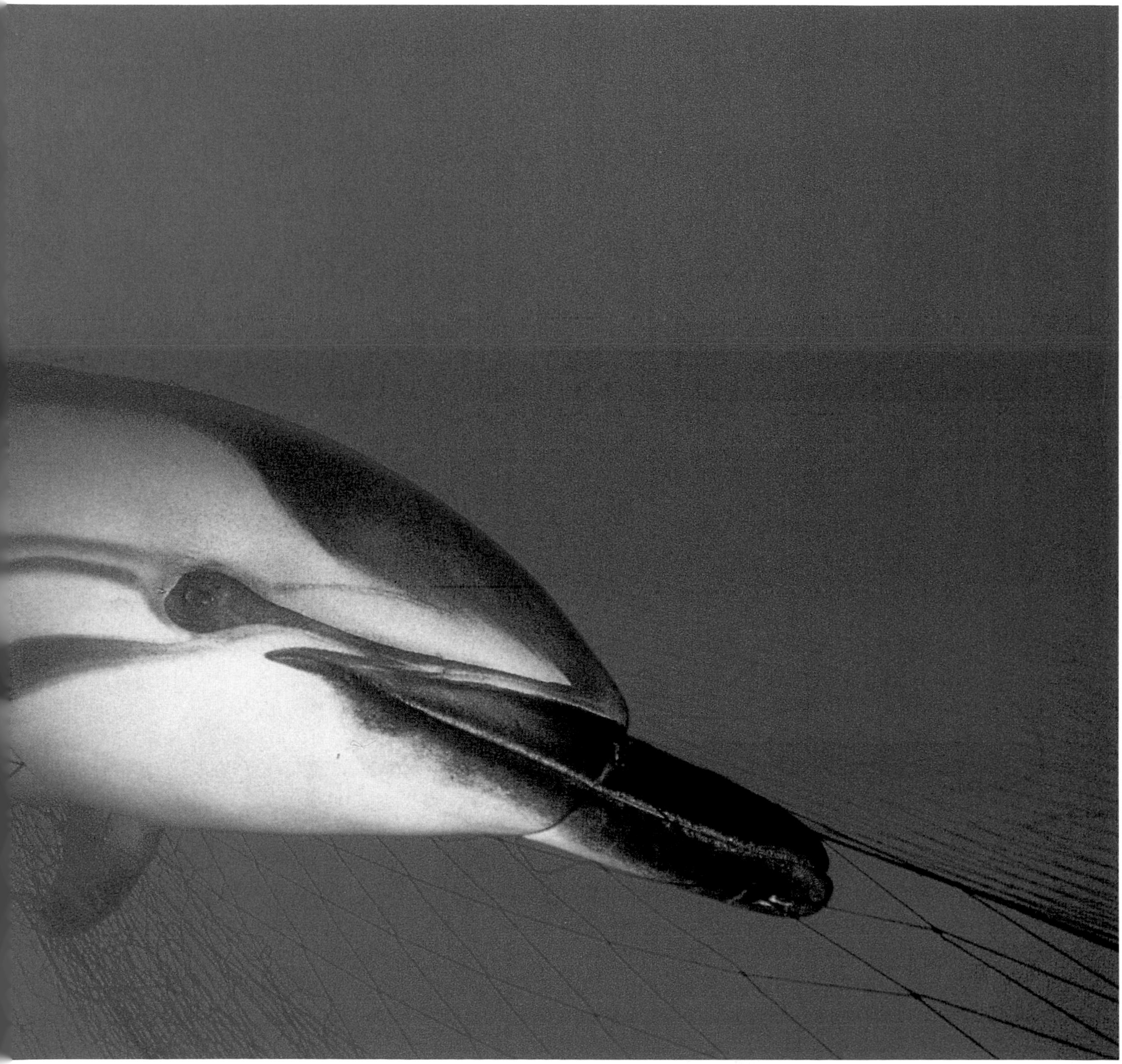

Liz Carr during removal of World Park Base, Ross
Island, Antarctica, 1992.
Robin Culley.

Athel Von Koettlitz, MV *Sirius*,
North Atlantic, 1982.
Pierre Gleizes.

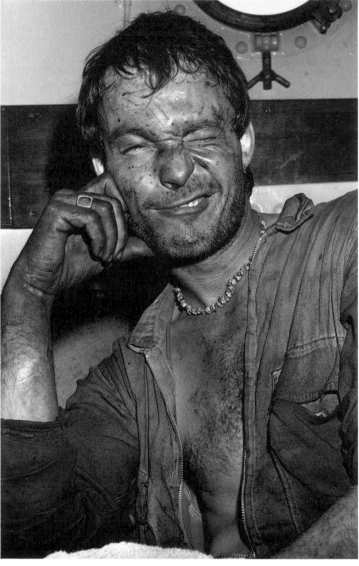

Action against whaling, Oslo, Norway, 1994.
Knut Falch.

Gavin smokestack climb,
Cheshire, Ohio, USA,
1984.
John Myer.

Crossing the Equator, South China Sea, 1994.
Mark Warford.

Climate action,
Frimmersdorf,
Germany, 1995.
Sabine Vielmo.

Toxic waste dumping, North Sea, 1983.
Fernando Pereira.

Sealing campaign, Newfoundland, Canada, 1982.
Pierre Gleizes.

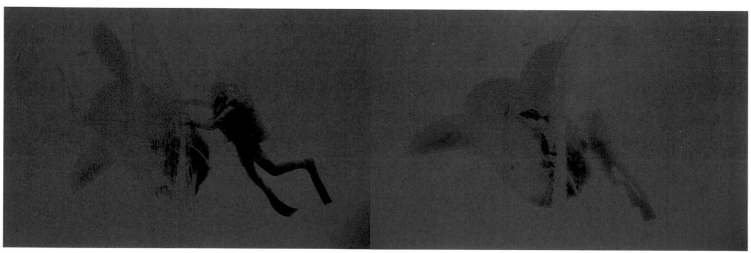

Greenpeace diver freeing sunfish from Japanese drift net,
Tasman Sea, 1990.
Roger Grace.

Overwintering in Antarctica, 1988.
Sjoerd Jongens.

Protest for release of MV *Sirius*, Cherbourg, France, 1983.
Pierre Gleizes.

MV Greenpeace, Southern Ocean, 1993.
Marty Lueders.

Rainbow Warrior and crew
escape from Spanish arrest,
Jersey, 1980.
Pierre Gleizes.

Awaiting action, *MV Greenpeace*,
Antarctic, 1990.
Robin Culley.

Press conference aboard
Rainbow Warrior,
Rarotonga, South Pacific, 1995.
Steve Morgan.

Crew members of *MV Sirius*,
1978.
Jean-Paul Ferrero.

Dolphin in drift net, North Pacific, 1990.
Roger Grace.

Burning oil wells, Kuwait, 1991.
Jim Hodson.

Maggie McCaw, *MV Gondwana*,
Antarctica, 1989.
Steve Morgan.

overleaf: Action against computer waste shipment,
Manila Bay, Philippines, 1994.
Mark Warford.

Radiation victim, Kiev, Ukraine, 1993.
David Sims.

Chernobyl nuclear power station, Ukraine, 1996.
Clive Shirley.

MV Gondwana,
Antarctica, 1989.
Steve Morgan.

Greenpeace inflatable
monitoring Japanese drift nets,
North Pacific, 1990.
Roger Grace.

Sampling, Antarctica, 1992.
Marty Lueders.

Storage point for contaminated equipment from Chernobyl,
Rassonka, Ukraine, 1995.
Clive Shirley.

Clearcutting of temperate rainforest,
Vancouver Island, Canada, 1993. Chip Vinai.

Logging in Siberia, 1993.
Steve Morgan.

Protest against transport of spent nuclear fuel,
Gundremmingen, Germany, 1993.
Sabine Vielmo.

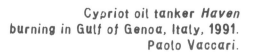

Cypriot oil tanker *Haven*
burning in Gulf of Genoa, Italy, 1991.
Paolo Vaccari.

Anti-nuclear demonstration, Koblenz, Germany, 1993.
Sabine Vielmo.

French drift net action, Vienna, Austria, 1994.
Wally Geier.

Log book, *Phyllis Cormack*, 1971.
Robert Keziere.

Greenpeace co-founder, Robert Hunter, on board the
Phyllis Cormack, 1971.
Robert Keziere.

Protest against transport of spent nuclear fuel,
Gundremmingen, Germany. 1993.
Sabine Vielmo.

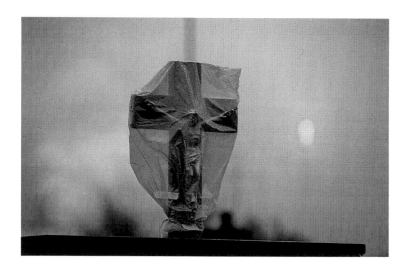

Gravestones protected from acid rain,
Cubatao, Brazil. 1992.
Steve Morgan.

Ken Saro-Wiwa,
Ogoni leader,
Nigeria, 1993.
Executed November 1995.
Tim Lambon.

Protest against the death
sentence of Nigerian anti-Shell
activist Ken Saro-Wiwa,
San Francisco, USA. 1995.
Melanie Kemper.

Honorary ceremony for crew of *Phyllis Cormack*, Alert Bay, Canada, 1971. Robert Keziere.

Robert Hunter and Ben Metcalfe on board the *Phyllis Cormack*, Vancouver, Canada, 1971. Robert Keziere.

The crew of the *Phyllis Cormack*, 1971. Robert Keziere.

opposite: Evacuation of Rongelap Island, South Pacific, 1985. Fernando Pereira.

Bridge blockade of
nuclear warship,
Golden Gate, San
Francisco, USA, 1988.
Sandy Scheltema.

Ricardo Roura aboard *MV Gondwana*, Antarctica, 1990.
Mike Midgley.

Evacuation of Rongelap Island, South Pacific, 1985.
Fernando Pereira.

Activists protesting NATO
nuclear capability,
Brussels, Belgium, 1991.
Kristien Buysse.

Greenpeace media crew,
Angra, Brazil, 1992.
Steve Morgan.

Greenpeace cameraman,
Tony Marriner,
Dingle Bay, Eire.
Paul Kay.

Anti-nuclear protest,
European Council, Brussels,
Belgium, 1993.
Luc Daniels.

The Dalai Lama visiting
Rainbow Warrior during UNCED,
Rio de Janeiro, Brazil, 1992.
Steve Morgan.

Ulrich Jurgens,
Captain, *MV Greenpeace*,
1990.
Steve Morgan.

overleaf: Handcuffed activists, Bethlehem Steel,
Baltimore, Maryland, USA, 1984.
Marc Osten.

Campaign against Brazilian whaling, Atlantic Ocean, 1978.
Campbell Plowden.

Golden Gate Bridge blockade, San Francisco, USA, 1988.
Sandy Scheltema.

Toxic waste shipment, Antwerp,
Belgium, 1992.
Wim Van Cappellen.

Damage caused by *Hurricane Andrew*,
Miami, Florida, USA, 1992.
Doug Perrine.

Dolphin alongside *Rainbow Warrior*,
Mediterranean Sea, 1993.
Marty Lueders.

Plutonium
production
demonstration,
Washington DC,
USA, 1987.
Tomas Walsh.

Blockade of oil tankers
entering Basel harbour,
Switzerland, 1995.
Dave Adair.

Banner hanging,
SS United States,
Istanbul, Turkey,
1993.
Tim Lambon.

Protest against
nuclear testing,
Mexico City,
Mexico, 1995.
Roberto Lopez.

Pipe block, Rotterdam, Netherlands, 1989.
Lorette Dorreboom.

Seal campaign, Madeleine Islands, Canada, 1980.
Deloffre.

MV *Greenpeace* crew member
in snowstorm during whaling actions,
Southern Ocean, 1995.
Roger Grace.

Protest against Trident missile test,
Cape Canaveral,
Florida, USA, 1994.
Colin Boyle.

Japanese factory ship, *Nisshin Maru*, Southern Ocean, 1992.
Robin Culley.

Swimmers in path of Japanese
whaling factory ship, *Nisshin Maru*,
Tasman Sea, 1990.
Tim Baker.

Gulf War demonstration,
Washington DC, USA, 1991.
Rob Visser.

Nuclear testing demonstration,
White House, USA, 1992.
F. Lee Corkran.

Anti nuclear testing demonstration at French consulate, Vancouver, Canada, 1995.
Josh Berson.

Baby Harp Seal, Newfoundland, Canada, 1982.
Pierre Gleizes

Nuclear weapons demonstration, Statue of Liberty, New York, USA, 1984.
Kurt Abraham.

Greenpeace solar unit, Los Angeles, California, USA, 1993.
Derrick Santini.

MV Greenpeace, Arndvoort Bay,
Antarctica, 1995.
Roger Grace.

Overwinterers' farewell, Ross Island,
Antarctica, 1990.
Mike Midgley.

Banner hanging, Mochovce power plant,
Slovakia, 1994.
Thorsten Hein.

New supplies for
World Park Base,
Ross Island,
Antarctica, 1989.
Steve Morgan.

USS Eisenhower, Palma, Majorca, 1988.
Miguel Gremo.

March into Frenchman's Flat (Ground Zero) to prevent nuclear test,
Nevada, USA, 1987.
Rocco Zappia.

Billboards against nuclear arms production,
Rocky Flats, Colorado, USA, 1990.
Jenny Hager.

Lloyd Anderson, Portman pipe block, Spain, 1986.
Lorette Dorreboom.

Falco dump ship, North Sea, 1983.
Fernando Pereira.

USS Eisenhower, Palma, Spain, 1988.
Miguel Gremo.

Demonstration against
French nuclear testing,
Canberra, Australia,
1995.
Glen Barry.

Blocking outflow pipe,
Portman, Spain, 1986.
Lorette Dorreboom.

Removal of World Park
Base, Ross Island,
Antarctica, 1992.
Tim Baker.

Inside World Park Base,
Ross Island, Antarctica,
1991. Tim Baker.

Blockade of US nuclear submarine,
Phoenix, Auckland, New Zealand, 1983.
Tom Donoghue.

Transport action, Uri Canyon,
Switzerland, 1987.
Lisa Schaublin.

Rainbow Warrior wreck,
Matauri Bay,
New Zealand, 1994.
Roger Grace.

Oil spill, Usinsk, Russia, 1994.
Mark Warford.

Spearfish caught in
Japanese drift net,
Tasman Sea, 1990.
Roger Grace.

Russian sailors, MV *Solo,*
Kara Sea, 1992.
Marty Lueders.

Baby dolphin killed by Japanese drift net,
Tasman Sea, 1990.
Lorette Dorreboom.

Dolphin caught in drift net, North Pacific, 1990.
Roger Grace.

Radiation victim, Rongelap Island, South Pacific, 1985.
Fernando Pereira.

Seal campaign,
Canada, 1976.
Patrick Moore.

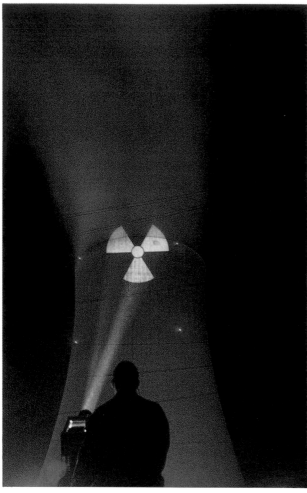

Projection on nuclear
power station, Gorsgen,
Switzerland, 1991.
Ruedi Staub.

Blocking outflow,
Fleetwood, NW England, 1992.
Jim Hodson.

Norwegian coastguard attempts arrest of Greenpeace inflatable,
North Sea, 1994.
Steve Morgan.

overleaf:
Bohunice nuclear power plant,
Czechoslovakia, 1991.
Veronika Leitinger.

Burning oil fields, Usinsk, Russia, 1994.
Mark Warford.

Norwegian whaling vessel *Senet*, North Sea, 1994.
Steve Morgan.

The *Rainbow Warrior*'s final resting place,
Matauri Bay, New Zealand, 1987.
Brian Latham.

AN IMPERATIVE TO ACT

What makes Greenpeace unique is its ability to catalyse change. Over the last twenty-five years, we have helped create an awareness that real change is possible. And we have done so through an imperative to act – not just to talk. Words alone cannot seize the public imagination – action can.

Campaigns like those on Brent Spar or against nuclear testing have been immensely effective precisely because they echoed public opinion so strongly. We cannot force improvement on our own, but we can help mobilise and inspire enough people so that it becomes irresistible.

In the coming years, we will face many new challenges. How to respond to globalization; the rise of the Asia – Pacific region; how to move politicians beyond their tired and destructive adherence to the philosophy of economic growth at any price. We need to address people's daily lives as consumers: to inspire them, not patronise them. To encourage them to recognise the power that their daily choices represent in shaping the world. We will need to seize their imagination as never before, to convince them that we can all live lightly on the Earth, while still enjoying life in all its richness.

Thilo Bode: Executive Director,
Greenpeace International